# THE
# SHETLAND
# SHEEPDOG

by Charlotte Wilcox

*Consultant:*
Mrs. Janice M. Leonard
LeoLair Shelties, 1961–present

CAPSTONE
HIGH/LOW BOOKS
an imprint of Capstone Press
Mankato, Minnesota

Capstone High/Low Books are published by Capstone Press
818 North Willow Street, Mankato, Minnesota 56001
http://www.capstone-press.com

*Library of Congress Cataloging-in-Publication Data*
    Wilcox, Charlotte.
    The Shetland sheepdog/by Charlotte Wilcox.
    p. cm.—(Learning about dogs)
    Includes bibliographical references (p. 45) and index.
    Summary: Introduces the history, development, uses, and care of this
popular dog breed from the Shetland Islands of Scotland.
    ISBN 0-7368-0162-6
    1. Shetland sheepdog—Juvenile literature. [1. Shetland sheepdog.
2. Dogs] I. Title. II. Series: Wilcox, Charlotte. Learning about dogs.
SF429.S62W55   1999
636.737—dc21                              98-37629
                                                CIP
                                                AC

**Editorial Credits**
Timothy Halldin, cover designer; Sheri Gosewisch and Kimberly Danger, photo
researchers

**Photo Credits**
Betty Crowell, 23, 35
Cheryl A. Ertelt, 6, 27, 36
Kent and Donna Dannen, 4, 9, 13, 17, 20, 24, 28, 31, 39, 40–41
Mark Raycroft, cover, 14, 18, 32
Unicorn Stock Photos/Les Van, 10

# Table of Contents

## Quick Facts about the Shetland Sheepdog

### Description

Height: Shetland Sheepdogs are 13 to 16 inches (33 to 41 centimeters) tall. Height is measured from the ground to the withers. The withers are the tops of the shoulders.

Weight: Shetland Sheepdogs weigh about 20 to 25 pounds (9 to 11 kilograms).

Physical features: Shetland Sheepdogs have long coats. This hair is thick and straight. Shetland Sheepdogs have longer hair on their necks.

| Colors: | Shetland Sheepdogs have five color patterns. These patterns are sable, tri-color, blue merle, bi-blue, and bi-black. Sable is brown, with black and white markings. Tri-color is black, with tan and white. Blue merle is gray with black spots, tan, and white. Bi-blue is gray with black spots, and white. Bi-black is black and white. |

## Development

| Place of origin: | Shetland Sheepdogs are named for the Shetland Islands. Shetland Sheepdogs came from dogs that lived on these islands north of Scotland. |

| History of breed: | Shetland Sheepdogs descended from farm dogs that came from Scotland and Norway. |

| Numbers: | The American Kennel Club registers about 35,000 Shetland Sheepdogs each year. To register means to record a dog's breeding record with an official club. The Canadian Kennel Club registers about 4,000 Shetland Sheepdogs each year. |

## Uses

Farmers and ranchers use Shetland Sheepdogs. The dogs protect farm animals. They help keep the farm animals together in a group. Shetland Sheepdogs also make good family pets.

# Chapter 1
# The Island of the Little Animals

Shetland Sheepdogs are named after the Shetland Islands. Shetland ponies and Shetland sheep also are named for these islands. Shetland dogs, ponies, and sheep have something in common. They all are small.

The Shetland Islands are a group of 100 islands. These islands are located in the North Sea. They are about 100 miles (161 kilometers) northeast of Scotland. They are about 400 miles (644 kilometers) south of the Arctic Circle.

People live on only 19 of the islands. The largest of these islands is called Mainland. It is

**Shetland Sheepdogs first came from the Shetland Islands in the North Sea.**

about 60 miles (95 kilometers) long. Some of the Shetland Islands are very small. Ponies, cattle, and sheep live on some of the smaller islands.

## Life on the Shetland Islands

The Shetland Islands are windy and rainy. The winters are cold and long. The time when crops can grow is short. Farm crops do not grow well there. Farmers raise animals instead.

Animals do not grow very large on the Shetland Islands. Shetland ponies are the smallest pony breed in the world. But they are stronger than any horse for their size. A tiny Shetland pony can carry a full-grown adult.

Shetland sheep also are small. They have special wool that protects them from the hard winters. It is the softest wool in the world. Sweaters made from Shetland wool are popular.

Farmers on the Shetland Islands use dogs to herd their ponies and sheep. Small dogs are good for herding these small animals. Most Shetland farmers use Shetland Sheepdogs for herding.

**Shetland Sheepdogs sometimes are used for herding farm animals such as sheep.**

## The Little Sheepdogs

Shetland Sheepdogs developed from other breeds of dogs. Some of these other breeds also could herd animals. They were easy to train. They did well in rough outdoor conditions. But the little Shetland Sheepdog is a breed of its own.

# Chapter 2
# Shetland Beginnings

The Shetland Islands' first herding dogs came from Scandinavia. This area later became the countries of Norway, Sweden, and Denmark. The people who lived there were the Norse (NORSS) people.

Many Norse people were farmers. They raised sheep, cattle, and horses. Norse people sailed to the Shetland Islands about 1,300 years ago. Some Norse people stayed on the Shetland Islands. They built homes and planted gardens. These farmers brought livestock and dogs from Scandinavia. They used dogs to help look after their livestock.

**Farmers sometimes use dogs to help care for their livestock.**

## Norse Dogs

Norse people used dogs to herd and protect farm animals. They also used dogs to pull sleds. These dogs were small to medium in size. They had thick coats to protect them from the cold. Many Norse dogs were all white or had white markings.

Norse farmers kept some livestock on the smaller Shetland Islands during the summer. They took these farm animals to the islands on boats. The livestock grazed on the islands. The farmers checked on the livestock only once in a while. The farmers also left some dogs on the islands for short periods. The dogs helped to look after the livestock.

These Norse dogs had several duties. They kept the farm animals together in a group. They kept the baby animals with their mothers. The dogs rounded up the livestock in the fall.

Farmers kept some livestock on the larger islands year-round. The farmers on these islands had gardens and fields near their houses. The dogs on the larger islands kept the

**Shetland Sheepdogs are smart, sturdy, and independent.**

livestock out of the gardens and fields. They kept the livestock from eating the crops.

These Shetland Island farmers did not need large dogs. Their farm animals were small. The farmers needed dogs that were smart, sturdy, and independent. The Norse dogs could take care of livestock by themselves. They could live in difficult conditions. They were just right for the job.

## Chapter 3

# The Development of the Breed

Life on the Shetland Islands changed about 1470. A Scandinavian princess married the king of Scotland. Her father gave a large gift to Scotland. He gave the Shetland Islands to Scotland as the marriage gift.

The Shetland people became citizens of Scotland. People from Scotland and England visited the islands. They liked the little ponies, sheep, and dogs they found there. They brought some of the dogs back to Scotland. Shetland farmers also received some herding dogs from Scotland.

**Shetland Sheepdogs have long hair that is similar to the long hair on collies.**

The Scottish herding dogs were called Border Collies. They were larger than the Norse dogs. Border Collies had shorter coats than the Norse dogs. People crossbred the Border Collies and Norse dogs. This combination of two different types of dogs resulted in a new dog breed.

## A New Breed

This new breed of dog had many names. In early days, these dogs were called toonies. "Tun" (TOON) is the Scandinavian word for farm. Later they were called Shetland Collies. By 1840, they were known as Shetland Sheepdogs. Many people today call Shetland Sheepdogs "Shelties."

This new dog breed changed a great deal from 1800 to 1900. Some breeders bred Shetland Sheepdogs with large collies. This produced larger herding dogs. But farmers did not want big dogs for herding.

Other breeders wanted to make the Shetland Sheepdog smaller. They bred Shetland Sheepdogs with toy-sized dogs. These tiny

**Border Collies are Scottish herding dogs. Shetland Sheepdogs descended in part from Border Collies.**

breeds included Pomeranians and toy-sized spaniels. Some of these puppies lost the sheepdog look. Shetland Sheepdogs were not bred with toy dogs very often after that time.

By the early 1900s, many people in the Shetland Islands and in England owned Shetland Sheepdogs. The first Shetland Sheepdog club began in 1908. The club started

**Many people like Shetland Sheepdogs for their looks.**

in the Shetland Islands. The English Shetland
Sheepdog Club started in England in 1914.

### Shelties in North America
Shetland Sheepdogs became popular in North
America during the 1920s and 1930s. Breeders
in North America bought dogs from breeders in
England and Scotland. The American Shetland
Sheepdog Association began in 1929. The

Canadian Shetland Sheepdog Association formed in 1988.

People like Shetland Sheepdogs for their looks. They also like the dogs' ability to protect and herd. Shetland Sheepdogs can protect people as well as livestock. Stories about Shetland Sheepdogs tell of this ability.

A Shetland Sheepdog won an award for heroic behavior in 1956. He helped save a young boy's life. A doctor had removed the boy's tonsils. That night, the dog was asleep in the boy's room. The boy started to bleed badly during the night. The dog awoke and ran to the bedroom of the boy's parents. He started to bark and pull on the parents' blankets. The boy's parents woke. The dog led them to the boy. The Shetland Sheepdog helped save the boy from bleeding to death.

The Walt Disney company made a movie about a Shetland Sheepdog in 1973. *The Little Shepherd Dog of Catalina Island* is the story of a Shetland Sheepdog who was lost. A farmer found him and took him to his farm. The dog later saved a horse that was going to fall off a cliff.

## Chapter 4

# The Shetland Sheepdog Today

Shetland Sheepdogs were very popular in North America during the 1980s. For several years, they were one of the 10 most popular breeds. In 1993, more than 40,000 Shetland Sheepdogs were registered. Currently the American Kennel Club registers about 35,000 a year. The Canadian Kennel Club registers about 4,000 a year.

Shetland Sheepdogs are loyal. They are especially good with children. Some Shetland Sheepdogs actually herd children to keep them

**Shetland Sheepdogs are especially good with children.**

together while they play. Shelties guard children against strangers. They bark at people they do not know. But after a warning bark, Shelties usually are friendly.

It is easy to train Shetland Sheepdogs. They are intelligent. They obey their owners. Shelties work hard. They can live on farms, in houses, or in city apartments. Shetland Sheepdogs are easy to care for. They get along well with people.

## Appearance

Shetland Sheepdogs look like small collies. They have long noses and brown or blue eyes. Some Shelties can have one brown and one blue eye. Their small ears fold over at the tips. They have long coats with extra hair on the neck. The hair on their tails is long and thick.

Shetland Sheepdogs can be many different sizes. They may be less than 13 inches (33 centimeters) tall. They may be more than 20 inches (51 centimeters) tall. A dog's height is measured from the ground to the withers. The withers are the tops of the shoulders. Most

**Shetland Sheepdogs are intelligent and easy to train.**

Shelties are 13 to 16 inches (33 to 41 centimeters) tall. They may weigh from 15 to 40 pounds (7 to 18 kilograms). Their average weight is about 25 pounds (11 kilograms).

## Shetland Sheepdog Colors

Many people notice the long coat of the Shetland Sheepdog. Shetland Sheepdogs are mostly shades of brown and black. These main colors can be five different patterns. All Shetland Sheepdogs have some white fur.

Sable Shetland Sheepdogs are brown with black and white markings. The brown can be light tan to deep red-brown. Tri-color Shelties are black with tan and white markings. Blue merle Shelties are gray with black spots, tan, and white. Bi-blue Shelties are gray with black spots, white, and no tan. Bi-black Shelties are black with white markings, but no brown markings.

Some Shetland Sheepdogs are almost all white. These dogs have dark hair on their heads. This color pattern is called color-headed

**Shetland Sheepdogs have five main colors. These three Shelties are blue merle, sable, and tri-color.**

white. Color-headed white dogs are not allowed in dog shows. Color-headed white is not an official color for Shetland Sheepdogs. But color-headed white Shelties usually are healthy dogs and make good pets.

Other Shetland Sheepdogs are almost all white. Their heads and their bodies are mostly white. These dogs are called double merles. These are Shetland Sheepdogs whose parents were both blue merles.

The white-coated double merle Shelties usually are not healthy. White-coated double merles can be blind or deaf. These dogs often have heart or kidney problems. They can have other health problems as well. For these reasons, white-coated double merles may not make good pets.

Tri-color and blue merle are two of the five main colors for Shetland Sheepdogs.

## Chapter 5
# The Sheltie in Action

Many Shetland Sheepdogs still are used for herding. These Shetland Sheepdogs herd many types of farm animals. These animals include sheep, cattle, ducks, and chickens. Shetland Sheepdogs also compete in herding contests.

Shetland Sheepdogs inherit the ability to herd from their ancestors. This natural ability is called an instinct. But not all Shetland Sheepdogs have a herding instinct. Even some of the first Shetland Sheepdogs were poor herders. Most Shelties are never tested for herding ability. A dog cannot learn to herd without some of this natural ability.

**Not all Shetland Sheepdogs have good herding ability.**

Dogs that have a herding instinct also need to be trained to herd. This is not the same as obedience training. During obedience training, dogs learn to follow such commands as sit, stay, and heel. Obedience training teaches dogs to pay attention to their owners. It teaches them to follow their owners' commands. Herding training teaches dogs to handle livestock. This training instructs dogs how to follow herders' commands to care for the livestock.

## The Shetland Sheepdog as a Stock Dog

Herding dogs are sometimes called stock dogs. Some stock dogs herd on farms and ranches. The Border Collie, Australian Shepherd, and Shetland Sheepdog are popular stock dog breeds. Shetland Sheepdogs usually are not suited for work on large ranches. They work best on small farms or ranches. Shetland Sheepdogs are good at handling small herds of livestock.

Some Shetland Sheepdogs that are stock dogs do not live on farms. But their owners

**Some Sheltie owners visit farms or ranches so their dogs can learn how to herd livestock.**

want their dogs to learn how to herd. They visit a farm or ranch on weekends. The dogs learn how to herd livestock. The owners learn how to work with stock dogs. Some owners enjoy this. It is good exercise for the dogs.

There are special clubs for stock dogs and their owners. These clubs hold contests and herding matches. The dogs can win prizes if they herd livestock well.

# Chapter 6
# Owning a Shetland Sheepdog

Shetland Sheepdogs make good pets. They are loyal to their owners. They get along well with people. Most Shetland Sheepdogs are healthy dogs.

### Feeding the Shetland Sheepdog
Kibble makes the best diet for many Shetland Sheepdogs. Kibble is dry dog food. It is the least expensive type of food and the easiest to store. Adult dogs eat kibble as it comes from the bag. This crunchy dog food helps keep dogs' teeth clean.

**Shetland Sheepdogs make good pets.**

The amount of food to feed a Shetland Sheepdog depends on the individual dog. An adult Sheltie may eat half a pound (227 grams) or more a day. Full-grown Shelties only need to eat once a day. Some people divide Shelties' food into two meals. Dogs must not be fed more than they need. Dogs that overeat can become overweight. This hurts their health.

Shetland Sheepdogs need plenty of water. They should drink as often as they want. Dogs should drink at least three times a day. They need fresh water every day.

## Grooming

Shetland Sheepdogs need to be groomed. To groom means to keep a dog neat and clean. Shetland Sheepdogs have long coats that shed. Dogs shed their hair when new hair grows. Shetland Sheepdogs should be brushed at least once a week. This helps keep the hair they shed off clothes and furniture.

Dogs do not need many baths. Dogs stay cleaner when people brush them. Dogs only need a bath if they get very dirty. Most

**Shetland Sheepdogs should be brushed at least once a week.**

**Shetland Sheepdogs need clean teeth. Dogs that eat kibble have cleaner teeth.**

Shetland Sheepdogs do not like to get wet. They do not like to take baths or to swim.

All dogs need clean teeth. Dogs that eat kibble usually have clean teeth. Chew toys for dogs also help keep their teeth clean. Many owners brush their dogs' teeth. They use special toothpaste for dogs. People must never give dogs human toothpaste. Toothpaste for humans must be spit out. Dogs cannot spit. They need toothpaste they can swallow.

Dogs need to be groomed in other ways. Dogs' toenails must be trimmed when they get too long. Their ears should be cleaned once a month. Veterinarians can show owners how to do these grooming tasks. A veterinarian is a person who helps sick or injured animals.

## Health Care

Dogs need shots every year to protect them from illnesses. They need pills to protect against heartworms. These tiny worms are carried by mosquitoes. They enter a dog's heart and slowly destroy it. Dogs also need a checkup every year for other types of worms.

Owners must check their dogs' skin for insects. They must check dogs' skin every day during warm weather. Some insects are especially harmful. For example, some ticks carry Lyme disease. This illness can harm animals and humans. Other problems come from fleas, lice, and mites. These tiny insects live on dogs' skin. They bother dogs and make their skin itch.

## Keeping Pets Safe

Dogs sometimes become lost. Lost dogs can be identified in several ways. A telephone number can be written on a dog's collar. A dog can be given a tattoo. This pattern in the skin is made of tiny drops of ink. Tattoos help owners recognize their dogs.

A microchip can be put under a dog's skin. This computer chip is about the size of a grain of rice. A veterinarian must put in the microchip. This microchip can be scanned by a computer. The computer will tell the owner's name, address, and telephone number.

## Finding a Shetland Sheepdog

Many people want to buy Shetland Sheepdogs when they are puppies. These people contact Shetland Sheepdog clubs in their areas. These clubs help people find good breeders. Good breeders raise healthy dogs to sell. Pet stores sometimes sell dogs with health problems.

**Shetland Sheepdog clubs can help people find a healthy Sheltie to buy.**

Some people find Shelties at rescue shelters. These shelters find homes for dogs. Usually, shelters have older dogs to adopt. These dogs usually cost less than those sold by breeders. Some are even free.

Shetland Sheepdogs are some of the best all-around dogs. They are easy to care for and handle. They are small but strong. They are watchful around strangers. But they are friendly and faithful to their owners.

**Ears**

**Withers**

**Muzzle**

**Chest**

**Forequarters**

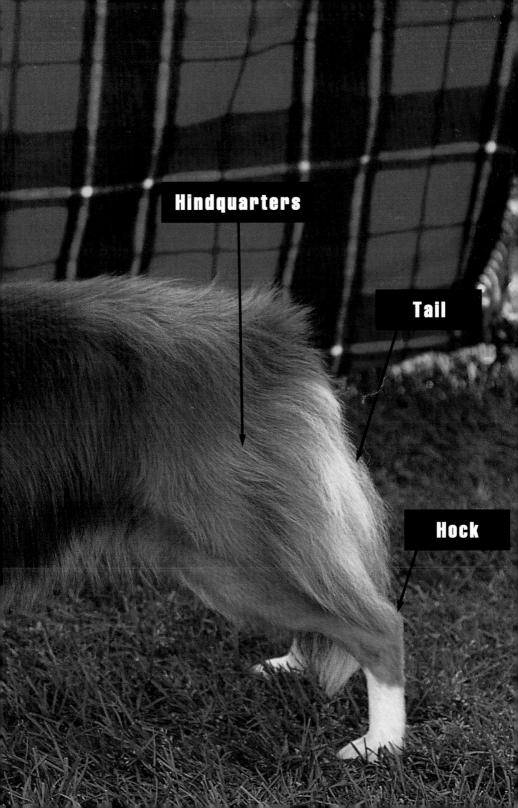

# Quick Facts about Dogs

## Dog Terms

A male dog is called a dog. A female dog is called a bitch. A young dog is called a puppy until it is 1 year old. A newborn puppy is called a whelp until it no longer needs its mother's milk. A family of puppies born at one time is called a litter.

## Life History

Origin: All dogs, wolves, coyotes, and dingoes descended from a single, wolf-like species. Humans trained dogs throughout history.

Types: There are about 350 official dog breeds in the world. Dogs come in different sizes and colors. Adult dogs weigh from 2 pounds (1 kilogram) to more than 200 pounds (91 kilograms). They range from 6 inches (15 centimeters) to 36 inches (91 centimeters) tall.

Reproductive life: Dogs mature at 6 to 18 months. Puppies are born two months after breeding. A female can have two litters per year. An average litter has three to six puppies. Litters of 15 or more puppies are possible.

Development: Newborn puppies cannot see or hear. Their ears and eyes open one to two weeks after birth. Puppies try to walk when they are 2 weeks old. Their teeth begin to come in when they are about 3 weeks old.

Life span: Dogs are fully grown at 2 years. They can live 15 years or longer with good care.

## The Dog's Super Senses

Smell:          Dogs have a strong sense of smell. It is many times stronger than a human's. Dogs use their noses more than their eyes and ears. They recognize people, animals, and objects just by smelling them. They may recognize smells from long distances. They also may remember smells for long periods of time.

Hearing:      Dogs hear better than people do. Dogs can hear noises from long distances. They also can hear high-pitched sounds that people cannot hear.

Sight:          Dogs' eyes are farther to the sides of their heads than people's are. They can see twice as wide around their heads as people can.

Touch:         Dogs enjoy being petted more than almost any other animal. They also can feel vibrations from approaching trains or the beginning of earthquakes or storms.

Taste:          Dogs do not have a strong sense of taste. This is partly because their sense of smell overpowers their sense of taste. It also is partly because they swallow food too quickly to taste it well.

Navigation:   Dogs often can find their way home through crowded streets or across miles of wilderness without guidance. This is a special ability that scientists do not fully understand.

# Words to Know

**coat** (KOHT)—an animal's fur or hair
**heartworm** (HART-wurm)—a tiny worm
carried by mosquitoes that enters a dog's heart
and destroys it
**kibble** (KI-buhl)—dry dog food
**Lyme disease** (LIME duh-ZEEZ)—an illness
carried by ticks that causes weakness, pain,
and sometimes heart and nerve problems in
animals and humans
**merle** (MURL)—speckled gray
**Pomeranian** (pah-muh-RAY-nee-uhn)—a very
small, long-haired dog from Poland
**register** (REJ-uh-stur)—to record a dog's
breeding record with an official club
**sable** (SAY-buhl)—a shade of brown

# To Learn More

**American Kennel Club.** *The Complete Dog Book for Kids.* New York: Howell Book House, 1996.

**Halpern, Monica.** *A Look at Dogs.* Austin, Texas: Steck-Vaughn, 1998.

**Rosen, Michael J.** *Kids' Best Field Guide to Neighborhood Dogs.* New York: Workman, 1993.

**Storer, Pat.** *Your Puppy, Your Dog: A Kid's Guide to Raising a Happy, Healthy Dog.* Pownal, Vt.: Storey Communications, 1997.

# Useful Addresses

**American Herding Breeds Association**
1548 Victoria Way
Pacific, CA 94404

**American Kennel Club**
5580 Centerview Drive
Raleigh, NC 27606-3390

**American Shetland Sheepdog Association**
3010 Sentinel Heights Road
LaFayette, NY 13084

**Canadian Kennel Club**
89 Skyway Avenue, Suite 100
Etobicoke, ON M9W 6R4
Canada

**Canadian Shetland Sheepdog Association**
26 Gorsey Square
Scarborough, ON M1B 1A7
Canada

# Internet Sites

**Best of Breed Online**
http://w3.mgr.com/mgr/howell/bobpages/

**Digital Dog**
http://www.digitaldog.com

**Dog Owner's Guide**
http://www.canismajor.com/dog/

**Herding With the Shetland Sheepdog**
http://sheltiehomepage.mcf.com/
    herdingwithshelties.html

**Sheltie Pacesetter**
http://www.sheltie.com

**Sheltie Rescue**
http://www.assa.org/shetland_sheepdog_
rescue.htm

# Index